Journey to Freedom

HALL OF FAITH SERIES

Journey to Freedom

PATRICIA MAXWELL

Pacific Press Publishing Association
Boise, Idaho
Oshawa, Ontario, Canada

Edited by Don Mansell
Designed by Consuelo Udave
Cover by Jim Padgett
Type set in 10/12 Century Schoolbook

Copyright © 1987 by
Pacific Press Publishing Association
Printed in United States of America
All Rights Reserved

Library of Congress Cataloging in Publication Data

Maxwell, Patricia, 1935-
  Journey to freedom.

  1. Knight, Anna, 1874-1972. 2. Seventh-Day Adventists—Biography. I. Title.
BX6193.K55M38   1987   286.7'32'0924 [B]   87-6988
ISBN 0-8163-0710-5

Contents

Chapter 1:	A Yen for Learning	7
Chapter 2:	The Cousin's Exchange	13
Chapter 3:	A Whole Bible—and More	19
Chapter 4:	Back on the Farm	25
Chapter 5:	Mount Vernon Academy	29
Chapter 6:	Battle Creek	33
Chapter 7:	Mission to Mississippi	39
Chapter 8:	Called to India	45
Chapter 9:	Calcutta and Karmatar	51
Chapter 10:	Providential Detour	57
Chapter 11:	Home Again in Mississippi	63
Chapter 12:	Later Labors	69
Chapter 13:	Honored at Ninety-seven	75

Chapter 1
A Yen for Learning

In 1863, President Abraham Lincoln issued his famous Emancipation Proclamation freeing "all slaves in areas still in rebellion," and in 1865 the Civil War ended, making it possible for that proclamation to become a reality for black Americans. Nine years later, Anna Knight was born.

Although her mother and Anna's brothers and sisters were no longer slaves, people were held in bondage by ignorance and prejudice. From her earliest years, Anna longed for knowledge. Over and over she expressed her desire in one recurring statement: "I want to learn all I can." In those days black children were not allowed to attend school with white children, and there was no school for blacks in Jasper County, Mississippi where she grew up.

Anna had no books of her own, so she turned to the white neighbor girls her own age for help. On Sundays, when she didn't have to work, she would visit them and ask them to show her their books. "Please teach me," she would beg. For a while they did, but they soon tired of helping her, preferring to play rather than teach a black girl.

Anna's parents were sharecroppers, paying for their land by giving a share of the crops they grew to a landowner until they had paid the purchase price. By hard, continuous labor, the family eventually acquired 160 acres this way.

The large Knight family all lived together in a one-room, hewn-log house with a porch on one side for a kitchen. Everybody had a job to do. When little more than a toddler, Anna carried a pail to the spring to bring water to fill the big wooden buckets at the house. She also carried jugs of water to the workers in the field.

As soon as she was old enough, Anna joined the workers in the fields, hoeing and chopping weeds with a heavy mattock. The farm consisted mostly of woodland, which had to be cleared. When not working the fields, Anna took her place at one end of a crosscut saw, felling trees and sawing logs. The logs were carried by pushing sticks under them, then lifting the ends of the sticks. It often took six or more persons to carry some logs, and Anna took her place at the end of the carrying sticks along with her brother or the other men. Some of the logs were cut into boards; others were split for rails.

"You are to work wherever you are needed," Anna's mother would always say. Anna preferred outdoor work, especially plowing, but she didn't neglect the housework either. There was always wool and cotton to be carded so it could be spun and woven into cloth for work clothes or knit into stockings and caps.

From sunup to sundown everybody in the family worked, and the hard work created large appetites, but there never seemed to be enough to eat. The family could seldom afford biscuits or bread made with flour; instead they ate corn pone, a kind of bread made of coarse cornmeal, water, and salt, and cooked in a Dutch oven or skillet.

"When I grow up," Anna's brother, Jim, would say, "I'm never going to eat corn bread for breakfast."

"Me either," Anna would agree. "I'm going to have flour bread at least once a day."

To help fill her stomach, Anna gleaned in the fields and forests, eating the nutlike tubers growing on the nut grass stalks and supplementing her diet with wild berries, wild grapes, persimmons, chestnuts, and hickory nuts.

Many times Anna walked six miles to the nearest store with her mother or grandmother, helping them carry a dozen eggs or a few chickens to exchange for sugar or coffee. A water-powered gristmill stood next to the country store, and

A YEN FOR LEARNING 9

here the Knight family brought their corn to be ground into meal for the following week's supply of corn pone. On rare occasions, they hitched up the ox wagon and drove thirty-eight miles to the nearest railway town. It took five days to make the round trip.

The struggle to survive on the homestead left little time for play or dreams, but Anna often straightened up from her hoeing and looked beyond the fields and woods in the direction of the white neighbors. Her eyes flickered with desire.

Then one day as she pushed the plow into the soil, creating waves of dark earth on either side of her, she suddenly stopped and spoke out loud. "That's it. That's how I'll do it." She thrust the plow deeper into the soil and strode purposefully behind it.

The next Sunday afternoon, she half ran, half walked through the woods to the neighbor's place. She paused on the doorstep to catch her breath, then knocked vigorously. The door opened. "Carrie, can you play with me?" she asked.

Carrie shook her blond head and said, "No, I've got to help mother with some spinning."

"I could help you," Anna offered, her voice edged with eagerness. "I'll do your spinning for you if you'll let me look at your books when I'm done."

"Sure!" Carrie responded. "I hate spinning, and if you're that anxious to look at my books, I'll even teach you a little out of them."

Anna seated herself and guided the wool into the spinning wheel with her fingers. The afternoon wore away, but she finished the job and turned to Carrie. "I'm ready to look at your books now," she said.

For more than an hour, she studied the pages, while Carrie helped her identify letters and words. The room dimmed as afternoon changed into twilight. "I've got to get home!" she said as she leaped up from the table and stepped toward the door. She ran through the woods and burst into her own house. The family already sat at supper. "Where've you been?" they asked.

Anna caught her breath. "Working wherever I'm needed—"

She grinned as they shot puzzled looks at her. "So I can be free—"

"Free?" Jim queried.

"To learn," she explained as she scooted a chair up to the table.

"Oh, so you're onto that again, are you?" he teased.

From then on, Anna spent Sundays and rainy days at the neighbors', trading work for time with books. Then one day, Carrie handed her a *Webster's Speller*. "Here, you can have this. I'm done with it." Anna grasped it, caressing the worn blue cover with her brown, work-rough hands. When the school year ended several months later, Carrie gave her another book: *McGuffey's Reader, Book Four*.

Whenever she could squeeze time away from work, and especially on Sundays when the family and neighbors would get together, Anna got out her books and organized spelling bees. Together, children and adults would choose sides and spell down. The two persons who stood the longest got to be captains over the next match. For hours at a time they would do this, until Anna became an expert at reading, spelling, and writing.

She also became the teacher for her younger siblings. She would nail boards together and paint them with wet soot. Then she would dig natural white chalk from the mud banks of the reed thicket so she could write on her "blackboard." The children would sit on the floor or on blocks of wood. She would give each of them chips of wood which they called "books."

"Hold your books in your hands," Anna instructed, "and look at me." Then she called out letters to them from ones she wrote on her "blackboard" with her mud-bank chalk. She alternated this with having them pronounce words from her *Webster's Speller*. They repeated letters and words after her until they had memorized them.

"Now, it's time you learned to write," she told them and led them to the yard, instructing them to copy in the sand the words written on her "blackboard." When they tired of learning, she gathered them into groups, and they practiced throwing stones at trees and stumps. The one who could hit the mark the most times was declared the winner of the game. She also introduced archery, giving them arrows which she made by driving nails into the ends of reeds, filing the nailheads into smooth, sharp points. They all became experts at archery and stone-and-stick throwing. But playtime never lasted very long before Mother would say, "Time to get to work now."

One morning, Anna stood on the porch pushing the butter churn paddle up and down.

"Your Ma home, Miss?" a man's voice asked.

Anna jerked her body around and faced a man mounting the porch steps, a leather satchel in one hand.

"Yes," Anna stammered, just as her mother stepped out the front door. The man removed his hat, bowed slightly toward Mother, and said, "I have something I'd like to show you, Ma'am."

Anna's mother invited him to sit in one of the wicker porch chairs while she pulled one up for herself. The man opened his satchel, pulled out a magazine, and held it toward Mother. She hesitated, then took it. Anna dropped the paddle in the butter churn and hurried to her mother, standing behind her, looking over her shoulder at the shiny, slick cover of the magazine the man held up.

"The Home and Fireside Magazine." Anna read the title aloud for her mother.

"Ma'am, I have a special bargain for you, today," the man said as he laid the magazine in Mother's lap and reached into his satchel and pulled out some pictures. "See these pretty pictures, Ma'am. Here's one of George and Martha Washington. Every American home should have a picture of our founding father in their home, don't you think so?" Before Mother could answer, he added, "And here's some more pretty pictures. You can have them all, plus the magazine for a whole year for only a dollar."

"Oh, Mother, get it please," Anna interrupted. Her mother looked back at her with a children-should-be-seen-and-not-heard look, but Anna ignored it as she stepped around to Mother's side. "I know you've got a dollar. We just sold some eggs yesterday. Please, Mother, please."

Mother's lips tightened, but she didn't say anything as she handed the pictures and magazine back to the salesman.

"This is a chance that doesn't come around very often, Ma'am," the man said as he took the materials and held them up with one hand while he opened his satchel with the other.

Anna begged once more. "Please, Mother, get it. I could read it to you. I know you'd like it. Please!"

Chapter 2
The Cousin's Exchange

"All right, Anna," Mother spoke, "I'll buy it. Go to the kitchen and get that dollar. It's under the sugar bowl."

Anna bounded into the kitchen, snatched the dollar from under the sugar bowl, hurried back to the front porch, and handed it to Mother, who in turn gave it to the magazine salesman. The man dug a pad out of his satchel and wrote up the order. "These pictures will come to you in the mail, and the magazine will be coming every month." He packed the magazine and pictures into his bag as he talked, then stood up and said goodbye.

As soon as the man disappeared around the first bend in the road, Anna clapped her hands together, jumped toward her mother, and said, "Oh, thank you, Mother, thank you!"

"Don't you ever beg for anything like that again," Anna's mother reprimanded, "Here you are a girl of fifteen carrying on like a three-year-old."

"But, Mother, I know you'll enjoy it. I'll read it to you in the evenings and on Sundays. I know I begged awful hard for it, but it—it—it means so much to me," she ended in a low tone.

Within a few weeks, the pictures arrived, and the magazine started coming each month. True to her word, Anna read the stories to her mother and the rest of the family. They looked forward to each issue, but to Anna, the magazines opened the door to knowledge and freedom.

Sometimes the magazine carried advertisements done in beautiful script writing. Anna admired the writing and carried the magazines outdoors so she could copy the script in the front yard. Using a pointed stick, she practiced penmanship in the sand, until she mastered writing.

One day a particular advertisement in the magazine caught Anna's eye. "Send ten cents," it said, "and get samples of books, papers, and catalogues." She had ten cents knotted in a handkerchief in a box under her bed. Quickly, she dug out her savings and hurried through the woods to ask Carrie to write a letter for her requesting the samples. Before long, she received a bundle of papers in the mail. She especially liked a magazine entitled *Comfort,* which she found in the collection. It cost twenty-five cents a year.

Anna picked cotton for a neighbor, earned the twenty-five cents, and sent for her subscription to *Comfort*. When the magazine started coming, it carried a column entitled "The Cousin's Exchange" in which people would make requests for things and get them from other readers. One of the requests read, "Will some of the cousins please send me some nice reading matter? I would like to correspond with those of my own age."

"What a great idea!" Anna squealed. She wasted no time in borrowing a pencil stub, sheet of paper, and envelope from Carrie. This time, she wrote her own letter, copying the request word for word, but inserting her own name and address, instead of the other person's. She mailed the letter and waited for answers.

Before long, the Knight box at the post office overflowed with books, papers, and magazines all addressed to Miss Anna Knight. Altogether, forty people sent her reading material. A large bundle of religious papers came from a man who wrote, saying that he was a Seventh-day Adventist colporteur in Texas.

"I wonder what a Seventh-day Adventist is?" Anna said to her brother, Jim, as he watched her leaf through the pile of reading materials.

"Who knows?" he answered.

"Whatever it is, here's another one," she said a bit later as she opened and read another letter. "This is from a Miss Edith I. Embree in Oakland, California," Anna explained to Jim.

"She says she's a Seventh-day Adventist and belongs to a group of young people who send literature to people. She saw my request in 'The Cousin's Exchange' and is sending me a magazine every week called *The Signs of the Times*. Think of that, Jim, a new magazine every week!"

But Anna found that she preferred reading the novels and story books she had received rather than the *Signs* and the other religious papers. She filled every spare moment reading the exciting tales contained in *Buffalo Bill, Wild Bill Hickok, Jesse James, Peck's Bad Boy,* and other books.

The demanding work of the farm didn't provide much spare time, and Anna couldn't keep up her correspondence with the people who had sent her things. Gradually, she didn't hear from any of them anymore, except Edith Embree. The *Signs* kept coming every week, and Edith always marked an article or two with a red or blue "X." Then, in a few days, a letter would follow.

"Be sure to read the articles I marked," Edith would write. "They were such a help to me, and I hope they'll help you. Write back to me and tell me what you think of them."

Anna couldn't ignore a request to express her thoughts, so she followed Edith's suggestion. Beginning with the front cover of the *Signs,* she would read every article, then write her thoughts in a letter to Miss Embree.

Sometimes Anna disagreed with an article or had questions about a topic, and she'd express her objections and questions in her letters. Edith wouldn't argue with her, but would write: "I'm sending you a tract of that very subject which will tell you all about what you want to know. If you don't understand it, ask me again; and I will be glad to try to help you understand."

Anna continued to study the *Signs* and correspond with Edith Embree. As time went on she spent less and less time with the novels and exciting stories she had previously loved.

One evening Anna looked up from reading a tract Edith had sent her and said, "I'd like to know more about this religion."

"We go to church whenever we can," her mother responded. "And we never work on Sundays. Seems like that ought to be enough religion to satisfy you."

"But it isn't, Mother," Anna answered. "I want to learn more. And all we have to learn from is that piece of the Bible you keep in the dresser drawer."

"Yea, remember that time I came in during that thunderstorm," Jim interjected, "and found you scared to death hanging on to that Bible piece and mumbling like you were praying?"

Anna was embarrassed. "You weren't so brave yourself," she shot back, "and besides, it helped."

Several weeks later, another storm swept through the neighborhood. This time, a tornado reached a whirling finger out of the black-green clouds and touched down three miles from the Knight home, injuring many people and killing others. The next day Anna walked through the devastated area, noting the twisted trees and shattered boards where houses and barns once stood. She shuddered and ran down the road to Aunt Helen's home. Without waiting for anyone to answer her knock, she rushed inside.

"Aunt Helen," she began without even saying Hello, "you're a Christian. Tell me: what if I'd been killed in that tornado. Would I be lost?"

"No," Helen answered, "if you got killed, you wouldn't be lost. If some of your people would pray for you and be baptized for you, that would save you."

"Does the Bible say that?" Anna asked.

"Sure," Helen replied. "I've heard preachers preach that lots of times."

"I don't want to hear what preachers say. Show it to me in the Bible," Anna demanded. Helen took down the family Bible, and the two of them walked out to the pasture, sat in a quiet spot, and hunted for the text. They searched for hours but never found it.

"I would have been lost," Anna concluded. "The Bible doesn't say anything about people getting another chance after they die." She paused and looked across the fields. "I've got to get a Bible and study this for myself. But how am I going to get a Bible?"

Helen shrugged her shoulders. "I don't know. But I think you ask too many questions. Why don't you just believe what the preacher tells you?"

"Because I don't want to be ignorant. I want to be free to think and learn for myself," Anna answered as she got to her feet. "I've got to go. It's time to milk the cow."

Not many weeks later, a "working" at the Chester farm was announced. A "working" was when neighbors got together and helped each other. From miles around, they would gather at a specified farm and put up a barn, roll logs, split fence rails, or work together on some other big project. The women usually quilted and prepared a large meal, which they spread out on a table in the yard. In the evening, everyone danced, played cards, and partied.

The Chesters had a lot of rails to split and a fence to put up around their pasture, so the neighbors called a "working" with a barn party and dance for the evening.

"Anna, we want you to lead out at the party," the young people said. "You're good at getting things going."

"I don't think I'll go this time," Anna answered.

"Not go?" they chorused in surprise. "Why not?"

"I just don't feel right about going," Anna said. "I've been reading in the *Signs,* and I don't think . . ."

"Forget your reading!" they interrupted. "You read too much. Come on! Have a good time!"

"All right," Anna agreed. "I'll go just this once. But don't ask me again, because I don't think it's the thing to do."

Anna barely danced once across the barn floor when a clap of thunder exploded overhead and a gust of wind slammed the barn door shut. Her feet slid to a stop. She jerked her head in the direction of an open window. Gray-and-black clouds looped and churned across the sky, punctuated by jabs of lightning.

As the storm boiled overhead, everybody quit dancing and moved to the center of the barn where Anna stood, stiff and unmoving. "I shouldn't be here," she finally spoke in a low voice. "I think God's warning me. I'm not going to any more card parties or dances."

"Anna, you're letting this religion stuff ruin your fun," one of the young men answered.

"I'm only trying to do what I've been learning," Anna replied.

"Well, just what is it you're learning?" one of the young women asked.

For several minutes Anna shared what she'd been reading and studying and how it had not only changed her thinking, but her day-to-day living—"but I've got so much more to learn," she added.

For the next six months Anna did learn much more as she continued to read and study the materials Edith Embree sent her. But one evening as Anna got out the piece of Bible in the dresser drawer, she sighed aloud, "I wish I had a whole Bible for myself!"

"I believe your Uncle Wesley has a Bible," her mother responded. "Don't think he ever uses it, either."

"Really, Mother?" Anna's voice brightened. "Are you sure? Do you think he'd let me use it? May I go over and ask him?"

"It's too far to walk this late in the evening, but you can go tomorrow after supper."

"Oh, I can't wait! I hope he'll let me have it. If he's not using it, don't you think he will, Mother?"

"I have no idea," Mother answered. "You'll have to wait and see."

Chapter 3
A Whole Bible—
and More

The next evening Anna walked to Uncle Wesley's homestead and found him in the back yard, chopping wood. "Uncle Wesley," she began, "Mother says you have a Bible."

"Yes," he answered without missing a stroke with his ax.

"Do you read it much?"

"Nope. None of us can read, except you and some of the other children."

"Well, do you suppose—" Anna cleared her throat. "Do you suppose I could have that Bible since I know how to read?"

Uncle Wesley anchored his ax in the chopping block and straightened up. He rolled his eyes upward as if looking for the right words. "Don't see how I could just give it to you. Book like that's worth something."

"Oh, I don't expect you to give it to me," Anna responded. "I'd be most glad to work for it. You must need to have something done around here."

"Yes, yes. There's lots of work around here, that's for sure." He paused again, choosing his words before he spoke them. "How about this?" he finally asked. "How about you picking 200 pounds of cotton for me in exchange for that Bible?"

"Yes, yes. I'll be glad to," Anna answered. "When do I start?"

Uncle Wesley laughed. "Tomorrow will be soon enough."

The next day, and every day until she picked 200 pounds, Anna was in Uncle Wesley's cotton field by sunup. When at last he placed the Bible in her hands, she wrapped it in a clean gingham cloth and carried it home. As soon as the evening chores were finished, she unwrapped the Bible, got out her back copies of the *Signs,* and compared the information in the papers with the Bible.

"Dear Miss Embree," Anna wrote after several weeks of comparing the magazines with the Bible. "I've got my own Bible now, and I've found that what your magazines teach is what the Bible teaches. But it doesn't agree with what the preachers around here teach. And, also, how is a person saved? If I got killed in a storm, I'm afraid I'd be lost, but I don't know what I have to do to be saved. Please answer soon. Respectfully yours, Anna Knight."

In the next week's mail, Anna received an answer from Edith Embree. "Please read the little book I'm enclosing, *Steps to Christ.* It will tell you better than I could how to be saved."

The next day, Anna gathered fat pine knots and stacked them in the chimney corner of the cabin. That evening, when the work was done, she sat on the floor next to the fireplace and read *Steps to Christ* by the light from the burning pine knots. Long after the rest of the family had gone to bed, she read the little book. She did the same the following two nights also. When she reached the last paragraph of the book, tears welled into her eyes, and she whispered, "God, I don't know how to pray, but I want to be saved, and I want to live like this book." She sat looking at the book for several more minutes, then closed it and got ready for bed. As she pulled the covers around her, she whispered again, "Thanks, God. I feel better now. I don't think I'll be scared of thunderstorms anymore."

A few days later, Anna wrote another letter to Edith Embree. "I finished the book *Steps to Christ.* It was just what I needed. I want to be baptized now and join your church."

In the next few weeks, Edith wrote to say she had contacted a Mr. L. Dyo Chambers of Chattanooga, Tennessee who would be writing to her regarding baptism. Before long, Anna got a letter from Mr. Chambers, and after some correspondence between them, he suggested she come to Chattanooga by train and be baptized at the Graysville Seventh-day Adventist

Church. He sent a picture of himself so she would recognize him when she arrived. Since she had no pictures of herself, he suggested she carry a copy of the *Review and Herald,* so he could recognize her.

When Anna told her family her plans, they objected. "You don't know what you're doing," they said. "You've lost your mind with too much reading."

Her mother especially disapproved. "Those people aren't going to be like what you read in their papers," she said. "You can't trust them."

"I know I've never met them," Anna answered, "but I've been reading and studying their materials for almost four years. I've checked it out with the Bible, and it agrees. If a person can't go by the Bible, what can you trust?"

"Well, I just don't like it, Anna," her Mother continued. "I don't know why you have to be so different from the rest of us."

"I'm not trying to be different, Mother, but I want to be baptized."

"Then we'll find a preacher here to baptize you. Why go running off clear to Tennessee? Why, that must be hundreds of miles from here." Anna's mother wiped her eyes with the corner of her apron.

"It's 382 miles," Anna said. "I looked it up. I don't want to be baptized by one of the preachers around here."

"And why not?"

"Because they don't keep all of God's commandments."

"Oh, Anna," her Mother sighed. "I'm convinced. Too much study has confused your mind."

"Mother, if you'll let me go for just a little while, I promise I'll come back and help make another crop next year. It's December, and not much can be done in the fields now, but I promise, I'll return for spring plowing."

At last Mother consented and Anna bought a train ticket with half of the money from the sale of a bale of cotton she and Jim owned together. Jim drove her in the ox wagon to the train station in Ellisville, Mississippi. "Sure going to miss you," he said as he stood beside her on the station platform. "How long are you going to be gone?"

Anna turned to him, her eyes sparkling. "I'm going to stay in Tennessee after I'm baptized and go to school."

"You never told us that."

"I know. But I've got to. I've never been to school before, and this is my chance."

"But you promised you'd help put in another crop."

"I'm keeping my promise. I'll be back in plenty of time." She dug some money out of her pocket and held it toward him. "See, I've saved half my money for a return ticket, so don't worry," she laughed, "I'll be home in time to beat you at plowing!"

When Anna arrived in Chattanooga, she had no trouble finding Mr. Chambers. He looked just like his picture, with a narrow face, full gray beard, and balding hairline. His blue-gray eyes showed concern as he helped her into his wagon. "How do you feel after such a long trip?" he asked.

"I feel fine," Anna replied. "I was scared at first because that's the first time I ever rode a train."

"You're a plucky young lady," he answered. "Tell me more about how you decided to be baptized." As they rode to the Chambers' home, Anna told him how her desire to be free from ignorance had led her to read and study any printed material she could find and how Miss Edith Embree had helped her by sending the *Signs* and other papers.

Before she could dismount from the wagon in front of the Chambers' home, Anna saw Mrs. Chambers open the front door. A short woman, smothered in a black coat, she walked quickly toward them, saying, "Welcome! Welcome! So glad to have you here!" A smile adorned her plain face, and her brown eyes glowed from behind small, round glasses. She hugged Anna. "You must be tired, dear, after such a long trip. Come in and let's get you a bite to eat."

The next week sped by for Anna. It was Christmastime, but it was also the Week of Prayer for the church. At the end of the week, Anna and two other young people were baptized in a creek near Graysville Academy a few miles north of Chattanooga.

She stood with the other baptismal candidates on the stream bank and watched two deacons chop a hole in the ice with picks.

"I don't care how cold it is," she said to her partners, "I can hardly wait to be baptized!"

After the baptism, church ladies bundled Anna and the others in blankets, packed them into a surrey, and drove them to the nearby girls' dormitory to get warm. As they rode along, Mrs. Chambers kept an arm around Anna's shoulders. Anna looked into her kind eyes and said, "I'm not worried anymore about being lost. If my name came up in the judgment, everything would be all right. I'm so happy!"

Mrs. Chambers squeezed her and said, "We're happy for you."

"You know there's only one thing that could add to my happiness," Anna said, "and that is if I could go to school."

"Well, we'll have to see what we can do to get you into Graysville Academy as soon as possible," Mrs. Chambers encouraged.

On Monday morning, at the age of nineteen, Anna Knight entered school for the first time in her life. She slid into a desk on the front row and never took her eyes from the teacher or the blackboard for the entire morning. During the lunch break, the teacher spoke to her. "The principal wants to see you in his office as soon as possible."

Anna found the office and entered. "Please sit down," the principal invited. "We're happy to have you here, Miss Knight. Please tell me about yourself. What schooling have you had?"

He listened carefully as Anna told about herself. When she finished, he said nothing for several minutes, then asked, "Are you a mulatto?"

"A what?" she asked.

"A mulatto."

"I don't know what that is, sir," she answered.

"A mulatto," he explained carefully and kindly, "is a person of mixed blood, part black, part white."

"Oh," Anna answered, "I don't know. It doesn't make any difference, does it?"

The principal shifted in his chair uneasily, shuffled some papers on his desk, then looked at Anna.

"It seems it does make a difference," he paused,"—to some

people. We are a Christian school here," he went on, "and we welcome people of all races. But there seem to be some folk in the town who don't feel the same as we do. They are very angry that we have admitted a black student to our school."

The principal looked down at his desk, then looked up again, shaking his head. "I hope you understand that it's not I, nor any of the teachers, who feels this way. We want you here, but perhaps because some of the townsfolk are so angry, you should wait until I can find out what you are."

"You mean I can't come to school here anymore?" Anna asked.

"I, er, we, the teachers, the church people want you here, but, but I'm afraid we can't do anything about the prejudice of the community."

Anna blinked her eyes, dropped her head, and swallowed several times, but still couldn't speak. Finally, she stood up and said, "Thank . . . thank you . . . for your trouble."

Her feet dragged and her shoulders sagged as she walked out of the principal's office and away from the school building.

Chapter 4
Back on the Farm

As soon as Mr. Chambers heard that Anna couldn't attend school, he promised to do something about it, and by evening he had. As they sat around the dinner table he explained it.

"I talked with Miss Jordan, the matron at the academy this afternoon, and she has agreed that you can stay with her and help her with her work, and she will give you private lessons. You don't mind working in exchange for learning, do you, Anna?"

"Oh no, sir. I'd be glad to. I've done that before. Thank you so much for helping me." She paused and blinked her eyes, "It won't be the same as going to school, but at least I'll be learning while I'm here."

Anna stayed ten weeks with the matron and worked and studied. By mid-March, it was time to go home and help put in another crop. When she arrived by train back at Ellisville, Jim greeted her. "How was school?" he asked.

"I learned a lot," Anna answered. But her family didn't like what she'd learned about being a Seventh-day Adventist. They ridiculed her about her strange beliefs and made it impossible for her to observe the Sabbath at home. So she worshiped in the woods. Each Sabbath, as soon as she prepared breakfast for the family and did her housework, she gathered up her Bible, lesson quarterly, *Review, The Youth's Instructor,* and other papers and headed for the woods. If it rained, she spent the day in the hayloft.

As the weeks went by, the ridicule from relatives and neighbors turned to threats, and Anna started carrying a revolver with her to the woods. As a girl, she'd spent hours riding through the woods on her horse and target practicing, and she had a reputation in the community as a good markswoman. After that no one bothered her during her Sabbaths in the woods or in the hayloft.

It rained a lot that spring and summer, making it difficult to plow the weeds between the rows of cotton. One Sabbath morning dawned bright and clear, however, and Anna's mother commanded, "You go plow that four-acre plot of cotton today."

"No," Anna answered. "Mother, you know I can't work on the Sabbath."

"You will work or I won't work," Jim broke in. "You lie around every Saturday and let the work go. I'll not work unless you do."

At this, Mother stepped closer to Anna, set her eyes firmly upon her, and commanded, "You will plow cotton today!"

Anna hesitated, her eyes flashed, and then she erupted, "All right! All right! I'll plow your field today. But if I don't get through today I'll finish it on Sunday. If I can't keep Sabbath, neither will I keep Sunday!" She turned and stomped out the door, slamming it behind her.

She harnessed the plow horse, jerking and slapping the lines across his back. He caught her mood and headed for the field at a fast trot, not slowing for the rest of the day. By sundown, they had raced over the four acres and finished the plowing.

Anna put up the horse and returned to the house.

"It's your turn for a bath," an older sister said as Anna entered the room.

"I'm not taking a bath tonight," Anna retorted. "No need for me to get cleaned up and dressed up for Sunday, because I'm working tomorrow."

"You wouldn't dare!" her sister responded.

"Oh yes, I would!"

The next morning, Anna put on her work clothes, grabbed a hoe, and headed for the flower garden.

"Anna, come back here! You can't work out there today!" her Mother called. "What will the neighbors think?"

Anna had already bent to her task and wouldn't look up. Soon the family packed themselves into the wagon and drove to

BACK ON THE FARM 27

church. They were so embarrassed by her actions that they didn't return till nightfall.

Anna sat at the kitchen table, writing.

"Dear Brother Chambers:" she began. "I don't see any point in trying to live a Christian life anymore. Today I got very angry. I haven't done that since I was baptized. In fact, everybody has noticed the good changes in me. But I sinned yesterday. I broke the Sabbath commandment and yelled at my mother. I've always obeyed my mother, but I don't know what to do when she says one thing and the Bible says another. Can you help me? I know I'm lost." She brushed a tear from her eyes as she folded the letter and put in into an envelope.

By Friday, she received a reply from Mr. Chambers. She carried the letter to the woods to read it. "God will forgive you," she read. "Tell Him you are sorry. He is waiting to forgive and restore you." Anna's eyes blurred as she read on: "The Bible says, 'Children, obey your parents in the Lord.' But only if the parents are in the Lord, and command us to do in harmony with His will should we feel obliged to obey. Read Acts 5:29. If you face this situation in the future, it would be all right for you to refuse to obey, if the command is contrary to the Lord's commandments."

For the first time all week, Anna smiled as she opened her Bible to Acts 5:29 and read: "We ought to obey God rather than men." She slipped a marker at the page before she closed the Book and knelt to pray. "God, please forgive me for losing my temper and for breaking the Sabbath. And help me in the future when my family speaks against me."

The future brought continual harrassment from her family, but Anna never again worked on the Sabbath. One day she approached her mother. "I'd really like to explain to you, Mother, why I keep the Sabbath."

"Don't you tell me anything!" her mother shot back. "Who do you think you are, trying to teach your own Mammy? I can't read, but I know one thing, young-uns aren't supposed to tell their elders what to do. Now, you listen to me. You either give up this Saturday-for-Sunday foolishness, or you can leave this house. I've had enough of your nonsense!"

Anna waited for her Mother to run out of words; then she

spoke: "All right. I'll leave, but I won't give up the Sabbath and my hope of eternal life."

"Then go!" her mother commanded.

"I'll go as soon as the crop is in," Anna answered. "I promised I'd do that."

"But Anna," her Mother's voice softened a bit. "You don't have to go, you know. All you have to do is give up these silly notions."

"I can never do that. I've got to obey God. You can take my horse, my cow, my cotton. Just give me enough for my railway fare to Chattanooga. You may have all the rest, except my Bible and a few personal belongings." Anna paused, then concluded, "I'm going out to get an education and be a teacher." She stopped, then added under her breath, "—and be free."

Not long after the crop was in, Anna wrote a letter to Brother Chambers, saying she was coming. She packed her few belongings into a homemade wooden box and Jim once again drove her to the railway station in Ellisville. After she bought a one-way ticket this time she had five cents left over. With it, she bought a coconut to eat on the way. Before the train pulled out of the station Jim helped her stow her box under the seat. Then he kissed her goodbye and said, "I know I'll never see you again."

"Oh, you'll see me again when I get my education." She tried to cheer him up. But he didn't say anything as he retreated down the aisle, jumped off the train, and stood on the platform waving to her.

The train began moving, jerked, then moved again. Anna pressed her face to the window and waved. As the train gained momentum and rolled away from the station, she continued waving, long after she could no longer see Jim. Finally, she dropped her hand slowly, looked back once more, then wiped her eyes with her palms. Turning forward in her seat, she let Ellisville, Mississippi slip out of sight.

Chapter 5
Mount Vernon Academy

Brother Chambers met Anna at the train station in Chattanooga the following morning. He shook her hand and said, "Welcome, Anna. Like we've told you in our letters many times, we want you to consider our home, your home."

"Thank you," Anna answered.

"We knew you'd be staying this time," he continued, "so my wife made a winter cape for you." He pulled a garment out of a cloth bag and handed it to her. She grasped it, turning the black broadcloth fabric over in her hands.

"Oh, it's beautiful!" she said at last as she caressed the quilted satin lining. "Thank you so much!"

"You'd better put it on before we go out and get in the wagon," Brother Chambers advised. "December's a bit chilly in Tennessee."

When they reached the Chambers' home, Mrs. Chambers met them at the door. Her arms enveloped Anna, and she kissed her cheek. "Come right in and make this your home," she said as she held the door open for Anna and Mr. Chambers. "We have two other girls here, but there's always room for one more."

That evening Brother and Sister Chambers discussed Anna's future with her. "There's still so much prejudice in this town," Brother Chambers said, "that I'm afraid you won't be able to attend classes. But you can live with us and help my wife with her work, and we'll do our best to get you into school as soon as possible."

Anna bit her lip and dropped her head, working her hands together in her lap. Finally she spoke. "I want so much to go to school. I want to be a teacher. But . . . but I'll wait. Thank you for letting me stay here."

Mrs. Chambers had plenty of work to do. A milliner and dressmaker, as well as a baker, she had also organized a group of women into a Women's Exchange. One of the leading grocery stores in town let the women display and sell their homemade bread, pies, cookies, cakes, and needlework. Four days a week, Mrs. Chambers arose at 4:00 a.m. to bake salt-rising bread to sell. Often she'd make as many as sixty loaves a day, and Anna helped her.

"With your help, Anna," she said, "we can make extra money so we can buy you clothes for school." And true to her word, she bought cloth and sewed clothes for Anna. Each time she'd finish a garment, she'd say, "Anna, I hope this will last you until the Lord comes."

One day Anna blurted out, "I'm afraid the Lord will come before I ever have a chance to go to school."

"Oh, I know it's hard, dear," Mrs. Chambers soothed her, "but we must keep working and trusting God."

Not long after that, Elder G. A. Irwin spent the night at the Chambers' home and listened to them tell about Anna's conversion and her desire to go to school.

"Why, she should go to Mount Vernon Academy in Ohio. People are less prejudiced up there than they are here."

As soon as they told Anna about this possibility she asked, "When can I go?"

They laughed at her eagerness and said, "Next September. We'll need to get the necessary money together first."

The next few weeks and months, Mrs. Chambers doubled her work, baking and sewing and stashing the money she earned into a jar on the kitchen shelf for Anna to go to Mount Vernon Academy. Anna worked hard right along with her. But one afternoon, she fled to the attic to cry. Finally, Mrs. Chambers located her.

"What's wrong?" she asked as she put her arms around the girl. "Did you get some bad news from home?"

"No."

"Are you homesick?"

"No."

"Have I hurt your feelings?"

"No."

"Then what's wrong?"

"Oh, Mrs. Chambers, you're doing so many nice things for me," Anna sobbed. "And I'm so poor. I can never repay you."

Mrs. Chambers hugged Anna closer. "You dear child, we don't expect any pay for what we're doing. We believe you'll make a great worker in God's cause someday. We've helped many girls get started in the Lord's work, and we're glad to be able to help you. Why, if we should die before Jesus comes, then our work will go on through you."

Anna dried her tears on her blouse sleeve and answered, "I won't disappoint you, Mrs. Chambers. I'll keep your work going on. I promise."

By September the Chambers had saved and solicited enough money for Anna to go to Mount Vernon Academy, but when she arrived at school, Anna found classes much more difficult than she had expected. Math class was especially hard because she didn't know the multiplication tables. For three days the whole class waited for her to catch on to how to do the problems. On the third day, the teacher stepped to the blackboard and explained in as simple a way as possible each step of the problem as he wrote it out for her to see. "Do you understand?" he asked when he finished.

"Yes," she answered.

"Finally!" one of the other students sighed.

"Thought she'd never get it," another mumbled.

"Me either," a third chimed in. "Hope we don't have to go through this all year." They hurried out of the classroom muttering their irritation with her.

Anna lingered until they had all left. The teacher waited too. "Don't be discouraged," he said. "Keep trying and you will make it all right; one of these days you'll be a Moses and go back south to lead and teach your people."

"I want to," Anna replied. "But I feel so dumb, and I'm holding back the rest of the class."

"Don't worry about that," the teacher encouraged. "You just keep trying."

Anna did just that. Sometimes it took her till two in the morning to get her lessons finished. Freedom from ignorance came hard, and overcoming prejudice was just as hard.

One afternoon Anna came upon a group of girls standing on the sidewalk, laughing and giggling. "Here comes that green girl from the South," one of them sneered.

Anna bit her lip, clenched her fists, and raised her chin. "Never mind," she said over her shoulder as she passed them. "Green things grow."

She later gained the respect of her school mates when she accompanied a group of younger students on an outing in the woods. She climbed apples trees and picked apples for the girls and knocked chestnuts out of trees by throwing stones at them. The girls were impressed with her outdoor skills and knowledge, and the word got around the academy that Anna Knight was not stupid, after all.

By the end of the year, Anna proved to everybody, including herself, that "green things grow." She earned A's in all but one of her classes.

As the students packed to go home for the summer, they laughed and told each other how glad they were for school to get out. But when one of them asked where Anna was going, she replied, "I wish I could stay here and study all year, but I'm going back to Tennessee and stay with the Chamberses.

When she arrived in Chattanooga, she found Brother Chambers in poor health. His wife drew Anna aside and said, "My husband is not well. It's taking all we have to pay for his medical care. I hate to tell you this, Anna, but we're not going to be able to help you anymore with money for your schooling." She paused and put her arms around Anna. "But we want you to know you're welcome to stay here in our home as long as you want."

"Oh, I'm so sorry, Mrs. Chambers," Anna said. "I'll work wherever I'm needed here in your home. And don't worry, I'll get back to school sometime, somewhere, somehow." She stopped, caught her breath and added quietly, "I don't know how I'll do it, but I will, God helping me."

Chapter 6
Battle Creek

As they sat around the dinner table one evening a few days later, Brother Chambers said, "Anna, I've just learned of an industrial school in Battle Creek, Michigan, where students can work and earn all their expenses."

Anna put down her fork and looked at him. "Really? Do you think I could go there?"

"Yes," he answered. "I know several people at Battle Creek. I'll write some letters of introduction and tell them about your lack of finances and that you need to work."

"Oh, I'd be glad to work all I can just so I could go to school," said Anna.

Within a few weeks, Anna arrived at Battle Creek and delivered Elder Chambers' letters of introduction to Dr. J. H. Kellogg, Professor W. W. Prescott, and Elder L. A. Hoopes. The letters had the desired effect, because in a matter of days she was enrolled in the industrial school with four hours of classes each day and six hours of work.

"You need three classes to finish your preparatory work before you can enter nurses' training at Battle Creek College," the registrar told her. "We're signing you up for English, general mathematics, and elementary bookkeeping. You'll need to report to the industrial matron, Mrs. Hall, to get your work assignment.

Anna waited a long time in Mrs. Hall's office. In fact, she and another girl were the only two left. Just as Mrs. Hall called Anna's name, a woman burst into the room.

"Mrs. Hall, I want two girls for the laundry right away," she announced. "Miss Aldrich has taken two of my best girls to wait on tables at the sanitarium!"

"There are only two new girls left," Mrs. Hall answered. "Here they are; you may have them."

The laundry matron turned and rushed out, sputtering, "New girls! I always have to take what's left."

Anna said nothing as she followed the woman. When they arrived at the laundry, the matron shoved a mop and pail in Anna's direction and showed her how to mop the room. Carefully, swiftly, but without comment, Anna finished the job and was given another task. Toward the end of the day, the matron told her, "You've done excellent work today. I wish all new folk could work as well as you. I'm very sorry for what I said earlier."

At the end of a month, the laundry matron asked Anna to take over the "box room." Her job would consist of boxing the clean clothes and having them ready for customers to pick up. It would mean she would be working ten hours every day instead of six, but she could do some studying while on duty. Anna found another benefit to the job too. She learned everybody's name and made many friends. Nursing and medical students hired her to do their ironing for them, paying her by the piece. In this way, Anna was able to pay all her expenses at the industrial school. But it meant long hours at work for the privilege of taking classes.

Anna roomed in a small cottage heated by a stove, and when she got off work at the laundry at ten in the evening, the cottage would be cold. The combination between working in the hot laundry all day, then walking across campus in the winter air to a cold room gave her tonsilitis. She dragged herself to classes and to work, barely able to talk.

When a nurse stopped by to pick up her laundry and heard Anna croak, "Hello," she said, "You don't sound very well. Come with me. We're taking you to the sanitarium."

Nurses quickly put Anna to bed and gave her treatments every three or four hours. Within twenty-four hours, she improved so much that she got out of bed and returned to work, not waiting to be discharged. By evening, the tonsilitis had returned, but Anna kept going. The next day, the same nurse found her working in the laundry and once again sent her to the sanitarium. As Anna checked in once more, the head nurse lectured her about taking care of her health.

"They're not going to admit you into the nurses' class," she threatened. "Any girl who doesn't know how to take care of herself can't be trusted with the lives of patients."

This time Anna took the nurse's words to heart. She stayed in bed until she was officially discharged.

By the end of the year, Anna had not only paid all her expenses, but she finished the three preparatory classes, making her eligible for the nurses' class being organized. She continued working in the laundry until they sent for her.

"Why didn't you come before to join the class?" one of the nursing instructors asked her. "What have you been waiting for?"

"Uh," Anna stuttered, "Uh . . . the head nurse told me when I had tonsilitis that I couldn't be admitted, because . . . because I don't know how to take care of my own health."

Puzzled expressions crossed the faces of the nursing teachers. Finally the head nurse laughed and said, "I didn't really mean what I said, Anna. I only wanted to make you realize that you needed to take care of your health."

"Oh-h-h," Anna sighed. "How do I sign up?"

"First, you must sign this statement," one of them explained and handed Anna a sheet of paper. Anna read it carefully:

"I desire to take nurses' training so that I can be a self-supporting missionary nurse. It is not my intention to be a professional nurse working only to earn money for myself." Without hesitation Anna reached for a pen and signed her name.

After she had completed the rest of the registration requirements, Anna was given two nurses' uniforms, two pairs of shoes, and the required books for the first year. She would be "on probation," working without pay as a nurses' aid, until she finished her theoretical training.

For her work experience, she was assigned to the strength-test room. The very first day at work, one of the instructors asked, "Do you know how to swim, Anna?"

"Yes. My mother taught me when I was just a little girl." Anna paused and her eyes grew blank to her surroundings. "I nearly drowned in a whirlpool in our creek. As soon as they got me revived, Mother put me right back in the water and started teaching me to swim. She said she didn't want me to be afraid or be a coward." Anna blinked and looked at her instructor. "Yes, I can swim."

"Good. I'm assigning you to the swimming pool for six hours a day to teach nurses and patients to swim."

Anna performed her job so efficiently that when she finished her probation period, they kept her in the strength-test department, but they gave her other responsibilities, as well. She had her own list of patients to care for in the treatment rooms and often got called to do relief work in other parts of the hospital.

Then one day the matron of the laundry became ill, and the manager asked Anna to come back to the laundry.

"I hate to give up my list of patients," Anna said.

"Well, I hope this won't be for long," the manager assured her.

"All right, then. If you really need me, I'll come."

"We really need you," he said.

When her classmates learned of the change in Anna's schedule, they said, "That's not fair! They shouldn't take you away from your patients and stick you back in that old laundry! You're supposed to be a nurse, not a washerwoman!"

"Well, I guess laundry work is also the Lord's work," Anna replied. "And I do know all about the job. Besides, my mother always told me, 'Work wherever you're needed,' and it looks like I'm needed in the laundry."

She didn't know how big the need was until she walked into the laundry and faced piles of dirty clothes stacked everywhere and a long list of orders waiting to be filled.

It took her three weeks, working eighteen hours a day, to get the work caught up. When she finally returned to the treatment rooms, her list of patients had been given to someone else, so Anna returned to the strength-test department and to teaching swimming.

Gradually, she got more jobs as a relief nurse, but her first five patients were mental cases. One woman, a maniac, had to have someone with her all the time. Anna got called in as a relief nurse one afternoon when the regular nurse had other duties to perform.

Following the instructions given to her by the regular nurse, Anna got the woman to the treatment room for her daily treatment without any incidents; but on the way out, the woman rushed at her, backing her against a wall. Anna refused to move, and the mad woman screamed, "You big old ox of a girl!" Then the woman turned abruptly and ran down the stairs, across the street, and into her own room, locking herself in. Anna ran after the woman, leaned against the door and knocked loudly. It didn't open, but the stomping and storming within echoed up and down the hall.

A callboy, hearing the commotion, hurried toward Anna, and she asked him to find a master key. He did and Anna opened the door. She stepped into the room, and the woman immediately pounced on her, pushing her against the door, slapping her face, and pinching her arms.

"For God so loved the world," Anna spoke quietly, "that he gave his only begotten Son . . ." The woman stopping hitting Anna and backed away. Anna repeated the rest of the Bible verse and went to another one. The woman sat down on her bed and listened. Anna continued reciting all the verses she could remember from Sabbath School and Bible classes. She had nearly exhausted her supply, when the regular nurse returned.

Anna told the nurse who relieved her what had happened. "At least it worked," she said. "The Bible verses worked just like you said they would."

The regular nurse nodded her head. "I know. It's really something how God's Word has such power!"

"Yes, it is," Anna agreed. "I'll never forget this experience!"

Anna got no more mental patients that year, but was given a variety of other cases to work with.

At the end of the year, Anna lacked 100 required hours of patient care. Her time in the laundry and the swimming pool had prevented her from getting the required hours and she was afraid she would not be allowed to go forward with her class.

In a note to her teachers she said simply: "I was always faithful to my post of duty, but I do not have the required number of hours. I leave it with you, praying that the Lord will impress you what to do."

Chapter 7
Mission to Mississippi

After a few days, Anna received a call to report to the head nurse. "We've gone over your record for the year and feel that you have been faithful to work wherever you were needed," the head nurse said. "You will not have to make up any time. You may go on with your class."

"Oh, thank you! Thank you!" Anna exclaimed.

She moved into her second year of training and was given a salary, with which she bought her uniforms, books, and supplies.

The months passed quickly, and as Anna's course in nurses' training came to a close, Dr. Kellogg called the class together for a special meeting.

"You have nearly completed your training at Battle Creek College," he reminded them. "It's my desire that when you finish here, you'll go out and become self-supporting medical missionaries.

"There's a great need in all parts of America, as well as foreign countries, for workers with your training," he continued. "Who will go?"

Anna raised her hand. Within a few days, she sat in Dr. Kellogg's office for an interview. "What do you want to do?" he asked her.

"I want to go back to my home in Mississippi," she said, "and start a school."

"Really?" Dr. Kellogg smiled as he spoke. "That's great, just great! Not many people would want to do that, but I'm glad you want to!" He paused, then asked, "What do you have with which to begin your adventure?"

"Nothing," Anna replied.

"Hm-m-m." He rubbed his chin. "We'll have to see about that. Well, you go back to work, and when we get some plans perfected, we'll call you."

Two weeks later, Anna entered his office again. Dr. Kellogg plunged into his plans at once. "We have your transportation all arranged. Our medical missionary society is taking care of that."

He picked a letter from the top of his desk and handed it to Anna. "Here's a letter. When you get to Cincinnati, give it to the ticket agent. He will sell you a ticket to Ellisville, Mississippi, at missionary rates."

Anna took the letter and held it in her hands as Dr. Kellogg talked. "I'm giving you a complete nurse's outfit; and, oh yes, here's another letter." He pushed papers around on his desk, found the other letter, and gave it to her. A $20 bill lay on top of it!

"Take this letter to the Review and Herald Publishing House here in town and get as many of my number one physiology books as you need. They'll charge the account to me. If you need more after you get to Mississippi and start your school, just let me know."

Anna studied the letters and money in her hand and started to ask, "What is the twenty dollars . . . ?"

Dr. Kellogg didn't let her finish. "The $20 is for your rail fare from Cincinnati to Ellisville. We've already bought your ticket from Battle Creek to Cincinnati. And the sanitarium will furnish your lunch for the trip. You may leave as soon as you like."

"Thank you," Anna said. "Thank you for your help and your trust in me."

"Well, God bless you, young lady," he said, "and may you have a safe trip."

That evening, a group of Anna's friends surprised her with a farewell party. "I can't believe I'm actually going to be a missionary nurse and a teacher," she told them.

"Like it or not, you are!" they kidded her.

"After six years," Anna answered. "I finally made it. You know, I've always wanted to be a teacher, so I could help other people be free from ignorance."

"Well, you've got your wish," they said.

The next few days passed quickly as Anna packed her things, said goodbye to her friends, and boarded the train headed south. She stopped in Chattonooga and spent a few days with Mrs. Chambers. Her husband had died while Anna was at Battle Creek.

Mrs. Chambers hugged her tightly and cried, "Oh, if Brother Chambers could only see you now! You've changed so much! Look at you, all educated and polished and improved. I can't believe you're the same girl who came to us six years ago!"

"That green girl from the South?" Anna queried as she laughed. "I told those Mount Vernon students that 'green things grow.'"

"You certainly have, my dear," Mrs. Chambers replied. "And I'm so happy, just so happy." She pulled a handkerchief from her pocket and wiped her eyes. "Now I know that our work will go on through you long after I'm gone."

Anna studied Mrs. Chambers' kind face. It bore more wrinkles than before, and the hair pulled back from her face in a neat bun carried more gray hairs. Her shoulders sloped more too.

"I promise you," Anna began, then had to swallow several times, "with the Lord's help, I'll do my best to carry on your work."

The few days in Chattanooga sped by, and soon the train carried Anna farther south. When she stepped onto the station platform in Ellisville, Jim ran to meet her.

"Oh, Sis!" he cried as he embraced her. "I thought I'd never see you again, but you've come back! You've come back!"

He stepped back and looked at her. "You've sure changed."

Anna laughed. "Maybe a little, but I bet I can still plow faster than you can!"

"Let's go home and find out!" he challenged as he picked up her baggage and loaded it into the ox-wagon. It took all day to make the twenty-mile trip home. When they arrived, Anna's mother greeted her warmly, as did all the other relatives and neighbors. Nobody said anything about her "strange beliefs." They actually seemed glad to have her home.

In a matter of days, Anna called all of her relatives and friends together and showed them the books, charts, and nurse's uniform which Dr. Kellogg had given her. "All this is to be used for the good of you and your children and for the community as a whole," she told them. "If you will cooperate with me, we can start a school. By working together, we can banish superstition and ignorance by letting the light of Christian education come in."

Everyone agreed to help, but all they could find for a school building was an old log cabin on Uncle Wesley's farm. Although it was too dilapidated for anyone to live in, it had a fairly good roof, two thirds of a chimney, and a usable fireplace. The walls, floors, and door all had plenty of cracks. The community felled a tree, split it, bored holes in it, and put legs into the holes to make two long benches which would seat about nine children each. Anna placed the benches in the middle of the room before the fireplace. To one side near the fire and the only window she put a homemade chair and table for herself.

When the weather turned cold, Anna closed the door to keep in the heat, but this made the room dark, so she threw pine knots into the fire to create more light by which to study. "This is how I used to read at home in the evenings by the fireplace," she told the children.

"Yes, my Daddy told me how you were always reading," a little boy spoke up.

In spite of the primitive surroundings, the children learned. They also worked. "It's good," she told them, "to work for your schooling." She paid them five cents an hour to cut wood for their fireplace. In the spring, Anna plowed up four acres of ground, and the children who could not afford to pay cash for their schooling, planted and hoed cotton. Their parents helped too.

In what few spare moments Anna could snatch from her busy life, she sketched plans for a new school building. A Battle Creek friend, Julia Luccock, stopped by one June day on her way to camp meeting in Iowa. When Julia heard of Anna's plans, she offered to get her father, who was a builder, to help. Within three weeks after she left, Julia sent back suggestions and detailed plans, plus $50 which she had solicited from people at camp meeting. Immediately, Anna called a meeting of all who might be interested in the school and told them of her plans to build a schoolhouse. She concluded by asking them to help. "If you don't have money, donate labor," she suggested.

They all promised to do something and promptly began felling timber, hewing the logs with their old-fashioned broadaxes. Anna joined them in making shakes for the roof while the women and children picked cotton on Anna's four acres. She sold the crop and added the money to the building fund. The cash was used to buy the lumber they couldn't prepare themselves, glass windows, a stove, and paint for blackboards. Within eight weeks, the building stood ready to receive students for a new school year.

Twenty-four enrolled in grades one through eight. Anna charged each pupil one dollar a month tuition. Only one could pay the tuition in cash. All the others paid theirs partly in cash and partly in labor. The labor consisted of clearing an acre of ground for an orchard and a vineyard. Working during part of their noon hours and after school, the children sawed logs into rails for a fence and for firewood.

Anna organized two Sunday school classes, six miles apart and taught the children that attended. Children in Graysville, Tennessee, sent their used Sabbath School papers for these missionary ventures. After Sunday School, Anna gathered the parents together and taught them to read and write. She also taught them how to cook better meals and how to can fruit. She stressed the need for better health practices and especially taught them about the evils of liquor.

Hanging her health charts on a wall, she showed the people what liquor drinking would do to their heart, liver, kidneys, and other organs. Convinced, they stopped buying "moonshine," the illegal liquor made and sold by "moonshiners." This angered the moonshiners, and one day, when Ann arrived at school, she found a note from them nailed to the front door. "We don't believe in women preachers," it said. "Stop preaching against our business, or we'll put *you* out of business."

Anna sent word back. "I'm not preaching," she wrote, "I'm only teaching and lecturing and will continue to do so. If you want to shoot, I'm ready."

"Anna," some of her friends pleaded, "you'd better stop your teaching against liquor, at least till these people calm down."

"I'm no quitter," Anna answered. "I'm going to keep on teaching the truth about this evil stuff. But if it will make you feel any better, I'll carry a gun with me."

From then on, Anna carried a revolver or double-barreled shotgun with her, keeping it near her in the schoolhouse.

She learned that the men who had threatened her, now started watching her on Sundays when she rode to and from her Sunday School classes, so she began going one way and returning another.

On her way home early one Sunday afternoon, Anna entered a lane about a quarter of a mile long that had a fence on either side and woods at the far end. She leaned forward and patted her horse's neck. "We've got to hurry home, Red, for my afternoon class," she whispered in his ear. As she straightened up in her saddle, she glimpsed forms staggering out of the woods and into the middle of the road at the other end of the lane. The sound of men's voices, raucous and profane, could be heard down the path and coming toward her. Anna shaded her eyes with one hand and strained to see better.

"It's them!" she whispered to Red as she dropped her hand from her eyes and gripped the reins. She kept riding forward, but the fingers of her right hand tightened around her revolver.

Chapter 8
Called to India

Anna guided her horse at a steady pace toward the end of the lane where the group of moonshiners waited for her. "All right, Red," she talked quietly to her horse, "do your stuff." She dropped the reins, threw up her hands, and slapped Red on his side. Red bolted forward and galloped toward the men, who scampered out of the way, yelling and cursing. From both sides of the lane, they fired their guns at Anna, but she ducked her head against Red's flying mane and urged him on faster. "Come on, Red, you can do it! You can do it!"

Red snorted, stretched out his neck, his hooves pounding hard and fast against the road, and sped out of range of the cursing and shooting moonshiners. Well down the road, Anna patted Red against the neck and calmed him down.

"You can slow up, now, Red. But you did great, just great. You didn't forget my signals, did you, old boy? You did it just the way I trained you years ago." The horse slowed to a trot and then to a walk as Anna continued talking to him. "But I think God is the one who brought us through that one. I prayed every second." She stopped talking to the horse and talked out loud to God. "Thank You, Lord, for Your protection. Now, please help me to keep Your work going here, so these people can be freed from superstition and ignorance. And help me be brave."

For several more weeks, the moonshiners continued their harrassment, but Anna refused to stop her work. She stood up to them, and gradually, as they saw that she was not afraid of them, they quit making trouble.

46   JOURNEY TO FREEDOM

In May, at the end of the school year, Dr. Kellogg asked Anna to come to Battle Creek as a delegate to the 1901 General Conference session. When she arrived she sat in the crowded auditorium and listened to the reports of the other delegates from all over the world. Then her name was called. She stood and said, "I praise God for what He's done in Mississippi in the last two years. We've established a school of twenty-four students; built a schoolhouse, free from debt; organized two Sunday Schools in two different communities and given many lectures on health and temperance; besides giving first aid and simple treatments to the sick." She took a deep breath and finished by saying, "To God be the glory!"

A chorus of Amens surrounded her as she sat down.

Between meetings, Anna renewed old friendships and made new ones. One day she found herself in a group of people listening to some nurses telling about the needs in India. "Right now," one of them said, "they're looking for two nurses to go to India."

Without hesitation, Anna spoke up, "If they'll send a man and his wife to look after my work in Mississippi, I'll go to India and stay there till the Lord comes."

Everyone in the group turned toward her with surprised looks on their faces. A man standing next to Anna finally asked, "May I tell the committee that?"

"Sure," Anna answered. "Tell them."

The next day a member of the committee approached her. "Is it true that you said you'd go to India?"

"Yes," she responded. "When I was in nurses' training here at Battle Creek, we fasted for two weeks one time, subsisting on a very limited diet and giving the money we saved to help during the famine in India. Ever since then, I've wanted to go to India. If you can find a couple to take over my work in Mississippi, I'll be glad to go to India."

"We'll see what we can do," he promised.

Within the next few days, all of Anna's friends heard about the possibility of her going to India, and they all offered advice. Some said she should go. Others said she shouldn't. She became confused and spent a lot of time crying over the matter.

Finally, one night she found a vacant room and knelt in prayer. "Lord," she began. "This world is Yours. The people in Mississippi are Yours as well as the ones in India. If You need me in India more than in Mississippi," she sobbed, "then take away this sorrow out of my heart and stop me from crying all the time about it." She turned and twisted the handkerchief in her hands, then dabbed her eyes with it. "If the sorrow and crying are taken away, then I'll know You are calling me to go to India."

She stopped crying, waited a few more minutes to see how she felt, and then hurried to find Donna Humphrey, a classmate who had also been asked to go to India. "Donna!" she shouted, "the Lord wants me to go to India! I just prayed about it, and He took away my crying and made me feel good about it!"

Donna's eyes widened. "Really?" she gasped. "I was just praying about what I should do, and the Lord has made it plain to me, too, that I should go to India!"

"Oh, how wonderful!" Anna laughed as she grabbed her friend's hands. "We can go together!"

From that moment on, Anna had no second thoughts about going to India. She shed no more tears, even when she said farewell to her close friends. The date of departure was so near at hand that she didn't have time to go home to Mississippi and tell her family goodbye. Arrangements were made for Anna's friend, Julia, and her new husband, to go to Mississippi and carry on the work Anna had begun.

The boat trip from New York to Bombay, India took thirty days. Traveling across the country from Bombay to Calcutta by train, took another thirty-six hours.

Both Anna and Donna were assigned work in the sanitarium in Calcutta, but Anna didn't remain long. One of the workers at the Karmatar mission station, 135 miles northwest of Calcutta, became sick and had to return to America; so Anna replaced him. Working with Miss Whiteis, the head nurse at Karmatar, she soon found herself doing a variety of jobs. Sometimes she extracted teeth or lanced boils. At other times she kept the accounts for the mission and taught Bible and English to the students in the training school. She also supervised the garden.

Anna tried to show the students how to prepare the soil for planting, but they balked, saying, "It can't be done that way in India."

With a pile of sweet potato slips at her feet, she gathered the schoolboys around her and said, "We've got to plant these." They tried to fulfill her request, but the ground was so hard they had to break it up with a pick.

"This won't do," Anna said. "Sweet potatoes will never grow in such hard ground. Get some gunnysacks," she instructed, "and the bullock cart. We're going to the river to get some sand."

With Anna's supervision they bagged river sand and hauled it to the garden spot in the bullock cart. There they added barnyard manure and mixed it with a mattock and spread it in trenches they dug in the ground.

"I remember seeing an American plow in the barn," Anna said to one of the boys. "Get it for me, please."

"No, ma'am." The boy shook his head. "Won't work. Might be all right in America. No good in India."

"Please bring it," Anna said in a firm voice, and he did. She hitched it to two bullocks and grasped the handles of the plow.

"Boys, get those animals going!" she shouted, but the bullocks wouldn't move. It took two boys to whip the animals into action. Anna gripped the plow handles with all her strength, pushed the blade into the soil and marched forward. The mission boys kept the bullocks moving by shouting continuously at them. Before she finished plowing, Anna's body glistened with perspiration, and her clothes stuck to her. But she didn't stop. Next, she gently pushed the potato slips into holes that she dug with her fingers in the freshly turned earth. The mission boys helped as best they could. It started raining, but Anna worked on.

When she finished the job, she returned to the bungalow, took a bath, ate dinner, and fainted. Indian helpers carried her unconscious body to her bed. "What shall we do?" the students asked each other in frightened whispers. "Miss Whiteis is gone to Calcutta to buy supplies. Who is here to help?"

"Send a telegram to Calcutta," one of them said, "and tell Miss Whiteis to come at once."

Two of the older schoolgirls stood by Anna's bed, waving palm fans over her and placing damp cloths on her forehead. Twelve hours later, a train came by, and they got some ice to pack around Anna's body. Finally she regained consciousness and looked up at the two girls standing over her, "What happened?" she asked.

"You nearly die," they said to her. "Make us very frightened."

"Oh-h-h," Anna sighed. "I must have become overheated." She breathed heavily. "I shouldn't have eaten so soon . . . so soon . . ." she gasped, "after bathing."

Anna got up within a few days, but was still very weak. Using the two girls as crutches, she hobbled outside, sat in a chair, and directed the boys in planting the remainder of the garden with turnips, cauliflower, tomatoes, beets, and other vegetables.

Soon, the garden produced a bigger harvest than anyone in Karmatar had ever seen before. "The missionary," the boys and village folk said, "she make a miracle with American plow!"

Anna told them, "No, I didn't make a miracle. God did." To the other missionaries, Anna added, "This is God's victory over superstition and ignorance."

When the hot season came, Donna Humphreys and Anna embarked on their first mission tour, traveling by train and tonga to the mountain resort of Simla. The tonga is a primitive vehicle with two large wheels having a board fastened to the axletree. Passengers sit back to back because there is no backrest. There are no springs or cushions, either, but Donna and Anna survived the trip and spent the season in Simla. They gave treatments, conducted a school of health at the YMCA center, taught Bible lessons, and sold Christian books and magazines.

The two young women enjoyed working together and became close friends. At the end of the hot season, they returned to Calcutta, Donna taking up her work in the sanitarium while Anna continued to sell books and give Bible studies among the English-speaking people.

A few months later, Donna suddenly became sick and died.

Her death came as a severe shock to Anna. She couldn't eat, sleep, or work. For days, she walked about the sanitarium with red, swollen eyes, hardly able to talk to anybody without crying. The mission superintendent, Elder J. L. Shaw, drew her aside one evening and said, "I know how heartbroken you are over Donna's death. Perhaps you should return to America until you've recovered from your loss."

Anna turned to him, a fresh spurt of tears springing to her eyes. "Leave here?" she asked. "Go home?"

"Yes," he answered. "You can't do your work here very well in your present condition."

Chapter 9
Calcutta and Karmatar

"Oh no, I can't go back home," Anna replied as she wiped her fingers across her eyes. "I feel I should carry on here and try to do her work as well as mine."

So it was decided that Anna would stay in India, working in Calcutta and Karmatar as needed.

After writing letters of consolation to Donna's sisters in America, Anna hopped on her bicycle late one afternoon to go to the post office. On the return trip at an intersection leading to a park, she turned her bicycle toward the park, seeking coolness and relaxation after a hot day. The sun had already set, and darkness crept rapidly across the grass and quiet street.

Halfway around the park, Anna spied a man on the roadside ahead of her. She pedaled faster, but as she passed him, he sprang into the road and tried to grab her. His movement didn't stop her, but it threw her bicycle off course and sent it hurtling toward a tree. The front wheel struck the curbstone, knocking Anna onto the ground with the bicycle on top of her. She scrambled to her feet yelling, "Police! Police!"

Nobody answered and the man lunged at her, his hands reaching for her throat. She punched him back with her fists, but he returned. This time, his fingers grazed her neck, catching the cord that held her watch and jerked it out of its pocket. The cord broke, and the watch fell to the ground. The man scooped up the watch, and Anna grabbed for it, but something sharp struck her right wrist, and her arm fell helplessly to her side. The man dashed off into the night, while Anna picked up her bicycle, struggled onto it, and pedaled home.

With bleeding hand, bruised face and bloodstained dress she entered her rooming house, amid a chorus of questions. "What happened to you?" everybody asked at once.

She told her experience and ended by lamenting, "He took my gold watch. The one Donna gave me!"

"You're lucky that's all that happened to you," they told her and proceeded to recount incidents of people who had been murdered in that same park. "It's not safe to be out alone after dark," they warned.

"None of this would have happened to me," she finally responded, "if I'd only listened."

"Listened?" they asked.

"Yes, listened," she repeated. "When I came to that intersection leading to the park, I heard a voice. It said, 'Go home now. You've been out long enough. It's time to go home.' But I didn't listen. It was so hot today, and the breeze from the park felt so cool. I didn't listen."

Nobody said anything, and Anna spoke again. "Believe me, I'm going to listen after this—and obey."

Anna continued selling Christian literature and giving Bible studies to interested people in Calcutta. She enjoyed her work, but one day she received a letter from home, bearing bad news.

"Mr. and Mrs. Atwood had to leave," the letter said. "Too many threats and violence . . . the schoolhouse burned. . . ."

Anna sobbed, "Why did this happen?" For a long time, she sat and cried over this apparent victory of prejudice over truth; then she dried her tears and wrote a letter to the General Conference, begging them to send someone to rebuild the school and continue the work in Mississippi.

Meanwhile, Anna continued working in Karmatar. One day, a group of Indians rode into the mission station in a bullock cart and asked for someone to return to their village and help a woman who had been sick for a month. "Our doctors cannot do any more for her. You come," they begged.

Miss Whiteis, the head nurse, got medical supplies together and asked one of the older schoolboys to go along to translate. Miss Whiteis rode ahead of the bullock cart on her bicycle, but before long she came back.

"It's a bad case of typhoid-malaria fever," she told Anna. "We'll need more supplies than I brought, so I'm going back to the dispensary to get them. Anna, you go on and get things started with the patient," she instructed.

When Anna and the translator arrived at the village, the people led them into a dark hut. Smoke from a charcoal bucket filled the air, and Anna coughed and blinked her eyes. When she became accustomed to the dimness around her, she saw an emaciated body lying on a coarse rice-straw cot. Only a thin cloth covered the woman's naked body. She had just had a chill, and someone had scooted the charcoal bucket under her cot to warm her.

Apparently, they had done this many times, for the woman's body was blackened by smoke. A spark had burned a hole in her back which had become infected. They had treated it by burning cow dung and sprinkling ashes on the sore.

"Please," Anna asked through her interpreter, "Please take the cot into the yard so I can see her better."

"Oh no. We can't move her," they answered. "To do so would be against our religion. It would make us unclean. You n e her. You are a Christian. You have no caste. You can't become unclean."

Anna and her schoolboy-interpreter got on either end of the cot and carried the patient into the yard. The woman looked as if she had never had a bath. Her tongue, swollen from lack of water, protruded between cracked lips. The villagers explained that their religion didn't permit them to give water to a patient with a fever.

Anna poured water from one of the jugs she had brought from the dispensary and started to wash the woman's face, but the people protested so loudly she had to stop. It was at this point that Miss Whiteis returned and asked what was going on. Anna explained the situation, shaking her head, and saying, "Such superstition and ignorance! I can't believe it!"

Just then the headman of the village strode into the yard and ordered the people to keep quiet. "You have failed to help her," he told them, "and you've asked the missionaries to help, so get out of the way and let them do whatever they want."

Miss Whiteis raised her hand and spoke to the crowd in a firm voice, "Step aside. Keep quiet and let us work."

But when she looked at the patient, she told Anna, "I scarcely know where to begin. This is a life-and-death case. I think we'd better begin with prayer." Together, she and Anna knelt beside the woman's cot and asked God to help them know what to do and to heal the sick woman, if it was His will. Then, they got up and went to work.

With warm water and glycerine, they softened the woman's lips and placed her tongue back in her mouth. They kept her lips moist with wet cotton and let her suck the water from it. They gave her an enema; then they washed her entire body, cleaning and disinfecting the sore on her back. They applied ointment to the sore and bandaged it. Finally, they placed a clean cloth under her to protect her skin from the rough straw-rope cot.

The woman couldn't speak, but she blinked her eyes and moved her lips slightly as if she was trying to thank them.

Before they left, Anna and Miss Whiteis gave the villagers bottles of water, stressing they must give the woman six or eight cups of it every day. They left medicine also.

Every day the woman's friends walked to the clinic for more medicine. After two weeks, they didn't come anymore, so Anna and Miss Whiteis went to check on their patient. As they rode into the village on their bicycles, the villagers crowded around them, smiling, talking, and pushing so close to them that the women had to dismount from their bicycles.

When they reached their patient's hut, she walked toward them, looking so healthy they couldn't believe it was the same woman. Even the ugly wound on her back had healed so well that not even a scar remained.

The villagers bowed to Anna and Miss Whiteis. "You have raised the dead!" they exclaimed.

"Oh no, we haven't," they replied. "Our God heard our

CALCUTTA AND KARMATAR   55

prayers and blessed our treatments. He healed her. Thank Him and worship Him. Don't bow to us!"

As the missionaries pedaled back to the mission, Anna exulted, "I'm so glad God won in that battle with superstition and ignorance."

"Me, too," her companion agreed.

This was a victory that resulted in the establishment of several schools and churches in that area.

Several months later, the mission sent Anna on her second missionary tour. This time her companion was a new convert, Miss Freida Haegert. The two planned to sell Christian literature in the towns along the rail line that crossed northern India.

One day the women came to an intersection and Anna suggested that Freida stay on the main line, while she took a branch line and worked the towns along it.

"It should only take two days, and then we'll join up again," said Anna. "Here you take the tiffin basket." The tiffin basket was the basket in which they carried food, cooking utensils, and a small stove.

"What will you do for food?" Freida asked.

"I'll find something along the way. It's only two days."

Freida's train left first: Anna approached the ticket counter to buy her ticket. But when the ticket agent found where she wanted to go, he objected.

"You can't go there. Only Indians live in that state. Foreigners don't go there. You might be kidnapped."

Anna insisted until the man finally sold her a ticket. She boarded an evening train and reached the town of Dhola long before dawn. Stepping off the train and entering the station, she located the ladies' waiting room and made a bed on a couch. About eight the next morning, she got up and walked outside to look at the town where she planned to sell books and magazines. She looked first one direction, then the other, but she couldn't see any town.

Retracing her steps into the station, she sought out the stationmaster.

"Where is the town?" she asked.

56 JOURNEY TO FREEDOM

"There is no town here," he answered. "This is only a railroad junction."

"When does the next train come?"

"Tomorrow morning. Same time you came today."

"Not till tomorrow?" Anna asked. "What shall I do all that time?"

Chapter 10
Providential Detour

Anna stood still in the middle of the empty railroad station for a few minutes with a concerned look in her eyes. Then she shrugged her shoulders and said, "Oh well, I'll write letters while I wait." She sat down, dug paper and pen out of her bag, and began. "I'm waiting for a train," she wrote. "Haven't had anything to eat or drink since last night. The water is too dirty here." She laid down her pen, got up, and approached the station master. "Sir, could you fix me some breakfast, please?"

He agreed and before long a servant brought a tray of rice and curry, but the rice had little stones in it, and the curry smelled of spoiled animal fat. The food was inedible, so Anna threw it away, then placed the price of the meal on the tray and thanked the servant who had brought it.

About noon a train pulled into the station and Anna dashed outside to meet it, but it was not going anywhere she wanted to go. As she returned to the station, she saw four men get off the train. The white silk European shirts they wore contrasted with their dark skin and hair. They strode directly toward Anna, their bare feet slapping against the plank floor. She turned her head away from them and tried to walk away in a slow, unconcerned manner, but they overtook her.

"Salaam [Peace to you]," they said. "Missionary?"

"Yes," Anna answered in a tentative voice while she twisted her fingers nervously around a handkerchief.

"Know Sahibs Lenker and Stroup?"

Anna's face relaxed. "Yes. Oh, yes. I met them several years ago. They were on furlough. Came to our school."

"Sahibs Lenker and Stroup sold us a wonderful book," the men explained. *Man, the Masterpiece* is the name. Do you have any books?"

"Yes, I do," Anna assured them and sold them *Heralds of the Morning* and the missionary magazine, the *Oriental Watchman*.

"Thank you, thank you," they said as they paid her for the books and magazines; then they asked if she would come to their state and teach. "We want to learn the way of these books. Our people need to learn. Won't you come?"

Anna explained that she couldn't come, but would take their request to the mission board. They boarded their train with friendly waves and reminders that she not forget to send them a teacher.

Anna sat in the station the rest of the day and that night slept again in the women's lounge. Early the next morning, she boarded the train that would take her to the next town. All morning it traveled through hot desert country, stopping about noon to change crew. Anna fanned herself with a paper fan and watched heat waves rise from the parched landscape. Tiring of the monotonous scene, she turned her face back to her train compartment.

Abruptly, she stopped fanning herself, blinked her eyes, and stared at the seat across from her. A white plate, piled high with brown toast, was on the seat. Beside it, a matching white cup contained a steaming hot drink. Anna stood up, opened the door to her compartment and looked both ways down the aisle of the train. She saw no one. Turning back to the meal before her, she picked up the cup and took a long drink. Then she reached for the toast. As she munched on a piece, she looked out her window again. A man stood on the platform just outside her window, wearing a uniform unlike any of the uniforms she had seen on any of the train crew. His eyes caught hers, and he spoke in perfect English.

"I hope you are enjoying your lunch."

She smiled. "I certainly am! I haven't had anything to eat or drink for a day and a half." She reached for the last piece of toast, and as she finished eating it, she heard the conductor call, "All aboard!"

Quickly, she pulled some rupees out of her purse, gathered up the plate and cup, and held them toward the man outside her window. But he was gone!

The train jerked away from the platform. She leaned out the window, looking in all directions, but still couldn't see the man in the unusual uniform, so she set the plate and cup back down on the empty seat across from her and stared at them.

"I can't believe this," she whispered. "Where did that food come from?" She closed her eyes. "Did you send it, dear God? Was that an . . . an . . . an angel? Oh, thank You, Lord, for taking care of my needs!"

By midafternoon, the train arrived at a junction where Anna would have to change trains and wait sixteen hours for another one to take her back to the main British line where she would meet Freida. When she got off the train and walked through the waiting room, a rough voice stopped her.

"Hey, lady, what are you doing here?"

She turned toward the voice and met the glowering eyes of the stationmaster. He swore. "What are you doing out here in an Indian state without an escort?"

She looked him in the eye and said, "I'm on the King's business, sir."

He snorted and swore again, the corners of his mouth curling up in a sneer, "Oh, I see! You're one of those silly missionaries trying to convert the heathen." He stopped for a minute. His eyes narrowed. "Say, do you believe there's a God?" He didn't wait for an answer but spat out the words, "I don't. I've been out here so long and seen so much, I'm an agnostic."

Anna didn't move while he continued to vent his antagonism. Then he stopped as unexpectedly as he'd begun. His shoulders sagged, and his eyes left Anna's face and looked out the window as if studying something a great way off. "I came out here to make money," he said, talking more to himself than to her. "I've made money but lost my religion. I used to be a Christian. My wife is a Christian."

His eyes moved back to Anna. "I wish she were here. She'd be glad to meet you." Once again, his gaze shifted to some unseen point. "But she's sick in the hospital in Bombay, I may never see her again."

Anna still didn't move. Neither did she speak. He looked directly at her again and asked, "Do you really believe there's a God?"

"Yes," she answered quickly, positively.

"Why do you?" he probed.

"Because of what He has done for me today."

His eyes turned hard and dark again, and the sneer returned to his face. "But what are you doing?" he demanded.

Anna pulled the book *Heralds of the Morning* and the paper *Oriental Watchman,* out of her bag and gave him a canvass. As she finished, he said, "I'll order both. Send them C.O.D. If my wife ever comes back, she'll love to have them."

"Sir," Anna urged, "I hope you'll read both of them too."

He didn't answer her question, but told her to make herself at home in the waiting room. She hired a coolie to look after her luggage, while she got on her bicycle to survey the town. But she found all the shops and bazaars closed. Finally, she pedaled up to the telegraph office and found two European women. They welcomed her with joy, asking her if she knew a Reverend Robinson.

"Two years ago," one of the women explained, "Reverend Robinson and his wife came through here selling a paper called the *Oriental Watchman*. We ordered it and enjoyed it so much."

"But the subscription has expired," the other woman interrupted, "and we don't know where to get it renewed."

"Yes, I know the Robinsons," Anna answered. "And I'm here taking renewals for that same paper."

The women paid for a new subscription, exclaiming over and over again how delighted they were that Anna had come by.

The next morning, Anna boarded the train and by afternoon was reunited with Freida. Both women chatted for an hour or more sharing experiences. "I was really scared, after you left," Anna admitted, "because the stationmaster told me how dangerous it was for a woman to travel alone in some of the outlying Indian states. But God took care of me. He even fed me! Can you believe it? Me, an ordinary person! He fed me just like he did Elijah!" She took in a quick breath and hurried on. "Then there were those four men. I thought sure they were kidnappers. But they wanted literature. And they want a teacher!"

Freida started to say something, but Anna couldn't stop. "That stationmaster was so gruff; then he ended up getting the papers for his wife, and I'm praying he'll read them too."

"Yes," Freida agreed.

"And when I rode my bicycle around that town and found everything closed up, I really wondered why God led me to that place. Then I found those two women! Oh, Freida, isn't it wonderful the way God leads us to people?"

"Yes, it is," Freida replied, "and I think we ought to thank Him for taking care of you, of both of us, on this trip."

Though Anna made a total of five missionary trips during her six-year term in India, this one would always stand out in her mind.

She loved mission work and always found more to do than there was time to do it in. Her co-workers sometimes told her to slow down, but she'd always quote her mother's saying: "Work wherever you're needed," and then would add, "—and there are certainly a lot of needs in India. I could stay here the rest of my life."

But letters from her family told of needs in Mississippi too. It seemed to be impossible to find anyone to rebuild the school and carry on the work she'd started there. She wrote again and again to friends in America and to the General Conference officers, begging them to find someone to go to Mississippi.

Then one day she received a letter written in childish script. It read: "Why don't you come back and teach us yourself? You understand us, and you are not afraid. Why would you stay over there, trying to convert the heathen while your own people here at home are growing up into heathen?"

Anna read and reread the letter, looking up with troubled eyes each time she finished it. Finally she folded it up. "I don't know what I can do," she said as she put it in the envelope and placed it in her desk drawer.

Chapter 11
Home Again in Mississippi

The letter lay in Anna's desk drawer for several days. Finally, she got it out, read it again, and wrote a letter to the General Conference officials. "Please send someone to Mississippi to teach my people," she begged. She concluded by writing, "If you can't find anyone to go, then please give me a furlough, and I'll go to Mississippi and do the work."

Months went by, and Anna kept working, giving Bible studies, selling Christian literature, treating the sick. Finally she got a reply to her letter. "We are happy to grant your request and give you a two-year furlough. You may go to your home and see if you can revive the work there."

Anna scurried to complete her work and pack her things, but before she left India, she wrote a letter to her family. "I'm coming home to start the school again," she wrote. "Please build another schoolhouse so it will be ready when I get there. Put it in the middle of the community," she instructed. "And build a less expensive building this time, so that if it's destroyed, it won't be so great a loss."

Since she intended to return to India after her furlough, Anna left her bicycle and some of her other belongings in Calcutta; then she boarded a cargo ship for America. Arriving in New York City, she bought a ticket to Washington D.C., where she visited the General Conference officials, getting their advice on how to conduct her work in Mississippi. From Washington, she traveled to Tennessee to see her old friend,

64 JOURNEY TO FREEDOM

Mrs. Chambers. But when she knocked on Mrs. Chambers' door, a stranger answered.

"Uh, uh," Anna stammered. "Doesn't Mrs. Chambers live here anymore?"

"She died two weeks ago," the woman replied.

"Died? Two weeks ago?" Anna was stunned. "No, it can't be!" Tears filled her eyes and spilled over onto her cheeks. "She was my best friend, the one who helped me go to school."

Sorrow choked Anna's voice, and sobs shook her body. The woman in the doorway reached out and touched her shoulder. "There, there now," she comforted.

Anna gasped and tried to speak, but couldn't. She just stood and cried. Finally, she raised her chin, bit her lips to stop them from quivering, and blinked her eyes. "I'll keep it going," she stammered. "I'll keep her work going. That's what she wanted me to do." Anna wiped her eyes with the back of her hands, turned, and walked away, headed for Mississippi.

Anna's family met her at the train station in Ellisville, escorting her home in a new spring wagon pulled by a span of mules. This was a great improvement over the ox wagon she had ridden in before.

The Monday after her arrival, she called a meeting at the schoolhouse. The whole community turned out to welcome her. Some of the very men who had helped burn the former school building sat in the audience and listened to her tell of her work in India.

She concluded her remarks by saying, "I've told you about my work in India so you'd know what it means for me to leave the work there and come home to try to help you. You people almost live in luxury compared to the people in India. Yet I know you need help too. So I've come back because you are my blood brothers and sisters, uncles, aunts, cousins, nieces and nephews."

"School will start Monday," Anna announced before she sat down. "Students, bring all the books or pieces of books you have."

On Monday morning, twenty-two students greeted her. The building was not completed, and as soon as classes dismissed in the afternoons, workers took up hammers and saws to finish the job.

The second Sunday after arriving in Mississippi, Anna resumed her Sunday Schools, conducting two classes in the morning in the town of Soso, six miles away, and one in the afternoon in her home. In a few months her relatives said they'd just as soon come on a Saturday afternoon.

After six months, nine of them asked to be baptized and join the Seventh-day Adventist Church. Her mother, two sisters, a niece, three cousins, and a man and his wife made up the group.

The conference president came; and on a Sabbath afternoon, the group met at the creek where Anna had learned to swim years before. "Shall we gather at the river?" sang the group. Their voices flowed together, and drifted across the water and through the woods. As the minister baptized Anna's relatives, she stood on the bank of the creek to embrace them as they came out of the water. When her mother walked toward her, dripping but smiling, Anna tried to speak, but couldn't. She clasped her mother's hands and looked into her eyes. "Blest be the tie that binds," the voices on the bank sang.

"Yes," Anna whispered as she and her mother walked up the bank together.

When school closed that spring, the conference president asked Anna to visit other churches and companies, giving Bible studies and encouraging the scattered church members in the state.

On one of her trips, she stopped to visit her aunt and uncle, Augusta and Horace Watts, in Sumrall, Mississippi. The first night, they kept Anna up all night asking her questions about the Bible. The next day, they invited their neighbors in for Bible study. All day and late into the next night Anna taught them from the Scriptures, stopping only long enough for meals.

When she left on Friday, Anna gave the Watts some tracts on the seventh-day Sabbath. The next day, Saturday, it rained so hard, the Watts couldn't work in their fields, so they studied the tracts and their Bibles. About noon, Augusta looked at

Horace and said, "I believe we ought to keep the Sabbath."

"I do too," he agreed. "Let's start right now."

Out of their commitment, a church and a mission school eventually grew, and Anna rejoiced that more of her family had broken out of their slavery to sin and entered into God's freedom.

As Anna's two-year furlough came to an end, she worked harder, visiting and encouraging the new believers, giving Bible studies, and teaching her school. In the evenings, she taught her younger sister, Grace, how to teach, so the school would keep going after she left.

People would often stop Anna and say, "If I had my way, I would not let you go back to India. We need you here. Let the white folk go to India. You stay here and work with us."

Anna would always smile and answer, "I know there are great needs here, but there are greater needs in India. Yet, I'll work wherever I'm needed."

One afternoon, the postmaster handed her a letter. "This one's from Atlanta. You sure know folks in a lot of places."

Anna read the letter as she walked home. "Dear Miss Knight:" it said, "The Southeastern Union Conference is starting a new sanitarium for black people in Atlanta. We need a medical matron to be in charge. Will you come?"

When she reached home, Anna spread the letter on her bed and knelt beside it. "Lord, you know I want to go back to India, but I'll go where You want me to go. So please show me Your will."

While she waited for some indication of what she should do, she kept working. But finally she wrote to the General Conference secretary, asking for his opinion. Within a few days she got an answer.

"We're trying to establish a strong work for black people in Atlanta," he wrote, "but it's very difficult to find trained workers. In fact, it's easier to fill a vacancy in India. We'd be delighted if you accepted the position as medical matron."

Anna prayed over this letter until she concluded God would have her go to Atlanta. It didn't take her long to pack her things and be on her way.

"Oh, Anna," her family said, "We're sorry you're going, but at least you're not going as far away as India."

"I hate to say goodbye too," she admitted, "but I'm happy that so many of you believe in Jesus, now, and that the school is going again. Keep up the good work that has been started here."

When Anna arrived at her new home at 209 Greensferry Avenue in Atlanta, Georgia, she found an empty, unfinished, and unfurnished house. She called one of the teachers at the small mission school and asked, "Is there some mistake? Is this where I am to live?"

"No mistake," the teacher replied. "That's it. Why don't you come and stay with me a few days, till you can find out what to do?"

The next day Anna bought a small two-burner gasoline stove and a second-hand bed. After a week of scrubbing and cleaning, her living quarters looked presentable and she moved in.

The treatment rooms at the nearby sanitarium were better outfitted than Anna's home. Equipment had been installed for hot-and-cold water treatments, electic-light baths, and physical therapy functions. The new sanitarium was ready to receive patients, but none came.

Instead, a man in uniform knocked on the door one morning and handed Anna an official-looking paper.

"What's this?" she asked.

"An injunction," he said. "From the mayor. You can't operate a sanitarium here."

"Why not?" she asked.

"Better take that up with City Hall," he replied. "I only deliver the notice."

"Well, I certainly will," Anna said as she closed the door. Wasting no time, she hurried to City Hall, where she discovered that a group of prejudiced people had circulated a petition against the sanitarium and had convinced the mayor to stop the medical work before it got started.

"But isn't there some way the mayor might reconsider this?" she asked the clerk.

"Sorry, Miss. It's the wishes of the people. They're the ones who got this petition up."

Back at the sanitarium, Anna walked through the treatment rooms, praying as she went. "Lord, I thought You wanted me to work in Atlanta," she said. "Now it looks like I can't. Here I am, up against prejudice again. What shall I do now? Please help me."

Chapter 12
Later Labors

Anna took the discouraging news to the conference officials, but she had a suggestion too. "Since we can't operate the sanitarium, why don't you let me operate a private treatment room in my home?"

"Sounds good," they said, but they also wanted her to take over the work of giving Bible studies to black people in Atlanta. A white woman had been doing it, but they thought it would be better if Anna did it.

She agreed and before long had many Bible studies going, but the treatment room work made slow progress. People seemed suspicious of water treatments, so Anna prayed that God would break down the prejudice and suspicion.

About this time, a neighbor woman got sick with a severe cold, and the doctors couldn't seem to get her well. Anna called on her and suggested that water treatments might help. "If your doctor wouldn't object, I'd be glad to come over and give you treatments every day," Anna offered.

"It's all right by me," the woman agreed, "if the doctor consents."

When the doctor came, Anna conferred with him, and he gave permission for the treatments. "I've done all I can do," he said, "you may as well try."

Anna gathered up her fomentation cloths and began treatments immediately. Several times a day, she immersed the woolen clothes in boiling water, wrung them out, wrapped them in clean towels, and placed the warm, steamy pile on the patient's chest. Within a few days, the woman could sit up, and in a week she was well. She delighted in telling her neighbors and friends about the miracle Anna had performed with "wet rags."

As a result of this experience, Anna made many friends in the previously hostile neighborhood. She found another avenue for witnessing in attending the graduation exercises of the black colleges in town. At these functions, she met many of the faculty, and when they heard that she had been the first black missionary to go to India, they invited her to come and speak to their classes about India. Anna accepted the invitations and made more friends and removed some of the prejudice against Seventh-day Adventists.

Meanwhile, the two-teacher mission school grew until another worker had to be hired. Besides the day classes, the teachers offered night classes to adults. Classrooms became overcrowded, and something had to be done to accommodate the interested people. To solve the problem, the mission asked Anna to be the school board chairman. The school had no money. Neither did the church, but the school needed more desks and a better stove for the larger room they had prepared for a classroom. Anna asked the conference officials for help.

"I'm sorry, Anna," they said. "Since this is considered a mission school, we're already paying 50 percent of the teachers' salaries. We can't do any more."

"Could I buy the stove and desk on the installment plan, then?" she asked. "We could make the monthly payments from the tuition that will be paid."

"Yes, you may do that," they agreed, "but you know you'll need money for a down payment, don't you? Do you have that amount?"

"Uh-h, no," she stammered. "No—I mean yes!"

Several of the men raised their eyebrows while others laughed. "Go ahead and see what you can do," they encouraged her as she left.

Arriving home, Anna headed straight for her desk drawer and pulled out a small, square tin box. She removed the lid, turned it upside down, and shook the contents onto her bed.

Pennies, nickels, dimes, quarters rolled out. She counted them and replaced them in the tin box, then hurried out of the house to the hardware store, where she selected a stove, made a down payment out of the money in her box, and promised to pay the rest in monthly installments.

From the hardware store she went to the school supply store. Telling of the needs of the mission school, she explained that she would like to buy desks with a small down payment and a small amount each month until they were paid for. After talking it over, they agreed to her plan.

The next day the stove and desks were delivered to the school "How did you do this?" the teachers and board members asked.

"The Lord did it," Anna said. "I used a little personal money for the down payments, and the conference officials gave me permission to buy on the installment plan. We'll make the monthly payments out of the tuition money we take in."

"This is quite a bit of debt," one of the board members said.

"Yes," another agreed. "What if folk fail to pay enough tuition, then what?"

"I believe the Lord worked this part out, and He'll take care of the rest too," Anna answered.

Some weeks later, as Anna sat at her desk answering letters, she came to one from Mrs. Edith Embree Runnels, the woman who had first sent her the *Signs of the Times* many years before. They had continued their correspondence through the years, and Anna wrote of her latest venture in Atlanta.

"We had to buy desks and a stove on the installment plan," she wrote. "I had saved some money for a winter coat for myself, but I used that for the down payment. I hope winter weather doesn't come before I can save enough again for a coat. But it's a real joy to give to the Lord's work."

Back came a reply from Edith: "I read your letter to our young people's group, and they suggested we take up an offering to refund the coat money. It is enclosed."

Anna stopped reading the letter and looked in the envelope and found a money order. Then she read on: "Another person in our youth group knew you back at Battle Creek College. She said she had a coat that had been given to her to pass on to some needy person. She's sending it by express mail so you can have it as soon as possible."

In a few days, the package arrived. Anna tore off the brown wrapping paper, opened the box, and folded the tissue paper back, lifting out a black broadcloth coat.

"Why, it looks almost new!" she exclaimed as she tried it on. "A perfect fit too. And a lot better quality than I could have bought."

"Thank You, Lord! —and You sent money besides! I can pay off the stove with that!"

Before long, the new school desks were all filled with students, and Anna had to hire two more teachers to teach the night classes. She, herself, taught English and physiology to the ninth and tenth grade students. In addition to academic courses, the mission school offered classes in first aid and home nursing. These night classes became very popular and won the interest and friendship of the community.

Besides her work with the school and the church, Anna's Bible studies increased until she gave an average of 500 Bible readings every year for the six years she lived in Atlanta.

Then church leaders called her to work in the Southeastern Union Conference, an area that included the states of Florida, Georgia, North and South Carolina, and eastern Tennessee. She headed up the educational, home missionary, and youth work for all the black schools and churches in this region. When she made her report at the end of her first year, the other workers expressed surprise at what she had done. As she traveled from church to church, she taught church members to keep records of their work for Jesus, and she did the same. She concluded her report by mentioning that she had written over 1500 letters that year.

"How did you do that?" someone asked.

"By hand, of course," Anna answered.

"I suggest," the union president said, "that each conference pitch in a little money and we buy Sister Anna Knight a typewriter."

"Would you please make it a portable one?" Anna asked. "I do a lot of traveling."

Everyone laughed and agreed, for they knew that Anna spent most of her time on the train, living from her trunk and suitcase.

Within a few years, Anna was asked to do the same work for the Southern Union, which included the states of Kentucky, western Tennessee, Alabama, Mississippi, Louisiana, and the western part of Florida.

At least twice a year, she visited the thirty-four black church schools. She always gave each student a yearly physical examination in addition to visiting and encouraging the fifty-four teachers in her area. In the evenings, she visited churches, going out on Ingathering singing bands, attending board meetings, or instructing the church members in how to give Bible studies. Whenever anyone commented about her many different duties, she'd smile and say, "I just work wherever I'm needed."

Year in and year out she kept up this busy schedule. In the summertime, she'd go to Oakwood College and teach summer school, and eventually she made her home there.

Oakwood College was always very special to Anna. She loved to tell how it got started.

"I was a young woman, living with the Chambers in Chattanooga," she said. "Elder O. A. Olsen and Elder G. A. Irwin stopped by and spent the night with the Chamberses. They talked that evening about a letter they had from Mrs. Ellen White. They even read the letter to us."

Anna relived the story. "Sister White said we needed to do more work for the blacks in the south. Naturally, my ears pricked up when I heard that!"

"The letter said a school should be started for blacks, and it should be located somewhere in the country near Nashville, Tennessee, or in northern Alabama. Elder Olsen and Elder Irwin talked a long time with Brother and Sister Chambers about this, and I listened and wished with all my heart there was such a school I could go to."

"The next morning before the two ministers left, we all gathered in the parlor for worship. Those two ministers spread Sister White's letter right out on the floor in front of them and prayed that God would lead them that day to the right property. "Why, they felt so strongly about it, that they cried, and their tears fell right down on that letter. I was deeply impressed. But you know, that very day the two men found a farm for sale near Huntsville, Alabama."

"They came out here," Anna would say as she pointed across the Oakwood College campus, "and found a torn-down fence and some shanty slave houses down there on the edge of the farm and the manor house still standing. They looked at each other and said, 'This is the place.' " Anna always paused at this point in her recollections.

"A few years after that, when I was a student at the industrial school in Battle Creek, they took a special offering to raise money to build a school for blacks. They asked everybody to give a dollar. Lots of folk didn't have a dollar, so they sacrificed a meal a day, saving the money for the offering the following Sabbath. That's how this school got here," Anna would conclude, "and I'm sure Oakwood College is God's school."

Anna's interest and contribution to Christian schools continued all her life. In addition to constantly traveling among the elementary schools, she founded a National Teacher's Association for black teachers.

She stayed so busy, "working wherever she was needed," that she rarely took vacations. For fifty years she gave herself to the physical, mental, and spiritual needs of people from India to Florida.

"Since 1911 I have kept an itemized record of the work that I have done," she reported when she retired in 1945. "I have held 9,388 meetings and have made 11,744 missionary visits. My work required the writing of 48,918 letters, and in getting to my appointments I have traveled 554,439 miles."

But she kept busy after retirement, too, writing a book about her life and teaching in a self-supporting school. After she retired the "second time," she devoted herself to what she called the "ministry of flowers," tending several flower beds on the campus of Oakwood College and supplying bouquets to teachers, students, and visitors.

Chapter 13
Honored at Ninety-seven

On November 17, 1971, people from all over the country gathered at Oakwood College to recognize the achievements of Miss Anna Knight. She was to be given the Medallion of Merit Award from the Education Department of the Seventh-day Adventist Church.

The hall filled early, with not a vacant seat left. A hum of conversation buzzed in the auditorium as friends greeted each other. The hum subsided into scattered sentences, then stopped altogether as the participants in the program filed onto the platform. People strained their necks to see around each other, all looking for the same thing.

Then they saw her: Anna Knight, ninety-seven years old, her shoulders a little sloped, her face lined with wrinkles, wisps of white hair showing beneath her black velvet hat, but walking with a determined step as one of the teachers she had taught to teach, escorted her to her chair.

The program began with a song, prayer, and comments by various educators. Anna's life story was told with tributes to her faithful and long service to Christian education. Finally, Dr. C. B. Hirsch, Secretary of the General Conference Department of Education, rose to speak.

"In the ninety-nine year history of Seventh-day Adventist schools," he said, "Miss Anna Knight is the thirteenth recipient of this medallion. It is presented to those individuals who make an outstanding contribution to Adventist education. This award of merit is the highest honor that can be given to an individual in the field of education by the Seventh-day Adventist Church. It is an honor, a privilege, and a pleasure for me to present to a distinguished educator and lady, this award, the Medallion of Merit."

Dr. Hirsch paused to open the small box containing the medallion. The audience sat, hushed, expectant, waiting. Dr. Hirsch removed the award from its case and looked at it as he continued to speak.

"This medallion reads," he said:

Anna Knight

for

Dedication to Seventh-day Adventist Education.

"Anna, will you please stand and receive this recognition from the church you served so long and so well?"

Anna's escort helped her out of her chair and walked beside her toward the center of the platform. Dr. Hirsch stepped toward Anna and slipped the medallion on its velvet cord around her neck.

The audience erupted into applause, wave after wave of it rolling forward through the room and engulfing the small, old lady standing in the middle of the platform. Tears ran unchecked down many faces as people continued to clap their hands together.

Anna looked out at them and shook her head in disbelief. She turned toward the other people on the platform. They smiled and clapped for her too. She faced the audience again as another rush of applause rolled over her.

Then she reached a wrinkled hand up to touch the medallion hanging around her neck. She bowed her head and read the inscription through watery eyes, while she traced the engraving with her thin fingers.

It had been a long time since those fingers copied script in the sands of Mississippi. A long time. She had struggled and broken out of the slavery of ignorance and prejudice and had helped scores of others—blacks, whites, and Indians—do the same. She was a woman who fought to be free and had won. But as she would say, "You do it by making Christ first and best in everything in your life and by working wherever you're needed."

Anna Knight died on June 3, 1972, seven months after she received the Medallion of Merit Award. She was ninety-eight years old.